REBEL *in a* DRESS

ADVENTURERS

BY

SYLVIA BRANZEI

ILLUSTRATED BY

MELISSA SWEET

SCHOLASTIC INC.
New York Toronto London Auckland
Sydney Mexico City New Delhi Hong Kong

To Mom and Daddy, Who Raised Four Rebels in Dresses. —S. B.

ISBN 978-0-545-45988-4

18 17 16 15 14   20 21 22/0

Printed in the U.S.A.   40

First Scholastic printing, March 2012

Cover design by Frances J. Soo Ping Chow
Interior design by Maria Lewis and Frances J. Soo Ping Chow
Typography: Helvetica, Just Me Down Here Again, Lady Rene, Mighty to Save, Pointy, Pea Bethany's Doodles, Sue Ellen Francisco, Trash Hand, and Trixie
Edited by T. L. Bonaddio and Lisa Cheng

CONTENTS

REBEL (n.):

One who is resistant to tradition,
one who attacks established beliefs,
someone who refuses to conform

"WHEN THE HISTORY OF WHAT
WOMEN HAVE ACCOMPLISHED IN
THE PAST IS IGNORED
OR
TRIVIALIZED,
EACH NEW GENERATION OF
ACHIEVING WOMEN MUST FIRST
REINVENT THE WHEEL."

—Janet Guthrie,
from *Janet Guthrie: A Life at Full Throttle*

The ladies you are about to meet are not comic book superheroes. They are real people, regular people just like you. Yet, each one is the stuff of legends. These women went above what is typical or expected. They didn't say, "I can't do that. I'm a girl." They did it, even if it was unacceptable for a lady of those times. They accomplished feats most men could not. They are not just amazing women; they are remarkable human beings. And that is why they are remembered. They are rebels. Rebels in dresses.

As a woman, I have no country...
As a woman my country is the WHOLE WORLD.
— Virginia Woolf

GUDRIDUR

BOLD

GUDRIDUR THORBJARNARDOTTIR

(Pre-1000-unknown)

Gudridur Thorbjarnardottir was the most traveled woman of her time. She made eight sea voyages. She lived in Iceland, Greenland, and North America. She walked across Europe, twice. And she did all of this around the year 1000. Her sea voyages were made in long Viking ships. Like sailors she used only the stars and landmarks for directions. This was five hundred years before

The Coming of the Norsemen in 1000 AD, tapestry designed and created by Mabelle L. Holmes, 20th century.

Columbus would set foot upon North America. Gudridur was adventurous. She was BOLD.

Eric the Red, Danish illustration from 17th century.

Gudridur's first voyage was tragic. When she was a young woman living in Iceland, Gudridur's father packed up their farm. He decided to move his family to Greenland, where Erik the Red's new

9

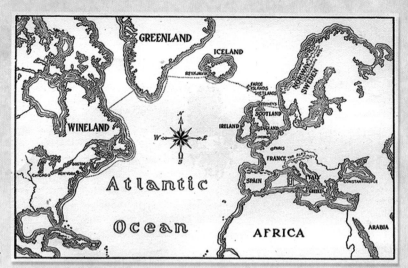

colony was settling. Gudridur boarded the long boat, along with her godparents.

The voyage was harsh; storms tossed the ship in the sea like it was a toy. Half of

the thirty settlers who had set out on the journey died, and both of Gudridur's

godparents were left behind in the sea.

After such a horrible trip, you would think

Gudridur would never want to sail again.

However, after only a year, she married Erik

the Red's son, Thorstein, and they set to

the seas. Their sights were on Vinland.

↳ Sculpture of Gudridur and her son, Snorri, by Ásmundur Sveinsson

Vinland

Scientists have uncovered ruins in Newfoundland, Canada, which show that Viking men and women landed there and stayed for a length of time.

"Love of learning is a pleasant and universal bond, since it deals with what one is and not what one has."

—Freya Stark, French explorer

Thorstein's brother Leif discovered it when he was blown off course. The land was filled with riches, such as timber, giant salmon, and wineberries. Thorstein and Gudridur headed west with a small crew, and again Gudridur found herself aboard a ship in a terrible storm. They got lost.

After months on a rugged sea, they saw land. Only they landed on the west coast of Greenland! They had wandered in circles for the entire summer. Since winter was coming, Gudridur and Thorstein stayed in the remote western part of Greenland with a farmer. Sadly, a fever spread throughout the land. The farmer's wife and Thorstein died. A widowed Gudridur returned home, only to find out her father had passed away while she was gone. Gudridur was now a widow *and* an orphan.

Gudridur remarried at Christmas—this time to a very wealthy merchant with royal blood. His name was Karlsefni. While most women stayed home to run the house and farm, Gudridur had wanderlust. According to the Icelandic Sagas, "Making a voyage to Vinland was all anyone talked about that winter. They kept urging Karlsefni to go, Gudridur as much as the others."

Detail of a Viking sandstone pendant featuring a Viking ship and fish.

Icelandic Sagas

The story of Gudridur was told in the two sagas, or epic tales, THE SAGA OF ERIK THE RED and THE SAGA OF THE GREENLANDERS. The stories were spread orally and written down over a century after Gudridur lived. In one saga, Gudridur was married three times, in another, twice. In others, she sailed with Thorstein, in another she just traveled with him around Greenland. But mostly, the stories of her adventures agree.

Gudridur set sail again with her husband and three ships of settlers. The voyage to the new land was calm. They found the shelters Leif Eriksson had left behind. Gudridur gave birth to a son in the land beyond the world. His name was Snorri, the first European born in North America.

Even with a young child, Gudridur was not to be left behind. She and Karlsefni left the settlement in Vinland (present-day Newfoundland) behind. They sailed south. Some think they arrived in Quebec, others believe New York. Regardless, they ended up in a land where butternuts grew and where the birds and the trees were not familiar. The land was good. There was plenty.

When the skraelings, or native people, arrived, it seemed like they might make good trading partners, but that soon changed. A fight eventually broke out. Soon after the skirmish, Gudridur and

"As a woman, I have no country....As a woman my country is the whole world."

—Virginia Woolf, novelist and essayist

her family returned to Vinland and then they eventually went back to Greenland.

Gudridur would not stay put for long—she and Karlsefni later sailed to Norway to visit the royal court. Gudridur had never seen such lavish living. But they didn't stay. They soon voyaged to Iceland and set up a farm.

After Karlsefni died, Gudridur left her son, Snorri, and his family in charge of the farm. She had one last trip in her.

Gudridur took a boat to Europe. Then she walked almost one thousand miles from Denmark to Rome, Italy. Her desire was to see the Pope in Rome. After her visit, she walked back to Denmark and then sailed to her home in Iceland.

Gudridur was finally done traveling. She returned to a church Snorri had built for her while she was on her pilgrimage. She went on to live there in worship.

Gudridur saw more than most women of her day, more than most people. She had traveled to the end of the world. Gudridur was a BOLD adventurer.

Around 1000

✷ The symbol zero is invented.

✷ Gunpowder is perfected in China for fireworks, not guns.

Gudridur Tidbits

✷ It was said that Gudridur had long hair that fell to her knees.

✷ Gudridur liked to wear pants under her long dress.

Champion

ALASKA

NOME

IDITAROD ROUTE

ANCHORAGE

I do not know the meaning of the word **quit.** Either I never did or I have abolished it.

Susan Butcher

ᴄSUSAN BUTCHER
(1954–2006)

While many women were cuddled comfortably in their slippers enjoying a warm cup of tea, Susan Butcher battled an Alaskan snowstorm with her dogs and her sled. The frigid winds whipped at seventy miles per hour, almost hurricane strength. The temperatures fell to negative seventy degrees Fahrenheit, colder than most thermometers even go. Susan got off her sled so the dogs could run better. The winds overturned the sled,

← A dog team racing in the Iditarod.

↖ Iditarod map showing Northern routes (even years) and Southern routes (odd years).

↖ Susan Butcher with lead dogs Granite and Sluggo.

"I do not know the meaning of the word 'quit.' Either I never did or I have abolished it."

—Susan Butcher

Susan jogs next to her sled as she leads her team to victory in the 1990 Iditarod Trail Sled Dog Race in Nome, Alaska.

but the dogs still pushed on. Neither Susan nor the dogs could see the trail, but the dogs found it again. Susan was doing exactly what she wanted. Dogsled racing is what she lived for.

Susan and her dog team were in the 1988 Iditarod, a dogsled race through the interior of Alaska that runs over one thousand miles. They had traveled over two mountain ranges, frozen rivers, dense forests, burned forestlands, and a storm that raged the Bering seacoast. Susan and her dog team were on the homestretch after more than eleven days in the barren wilderness. She turned the final bend and mushed toward Front Street. As Susan's red snowsuit came into view, thousands of fans cheered, bells

Susan Butcher at home with her dogs, 1990.

rang, and sirens blared. She crossed the finish line in Nome, Alaska, on March 16, 1988, at 8:41 a.m. It was her third win in a row; the first musher to ever have three consecutive wins! Susan Butcher was a CHAMPION!

This was Susan's eleventh Iditarod race. She placed nineteenth on her first attempt in 1978. She came back to race again every year.

Susan was ready for a win in the 1985 Iditarod. However, early in the race, Susan and her dogs came across a hungry, pregnant moose. The 1,000-pound animal became enraged, killed two dogs, and wounded ten others. Susan tried to fight off the moose, but it wouldn't leave. A fellow musher came upon the scene and helped Susan fend off the wild animal. Susan and her dogs dropped out of the race and went home.

Instead of giving up, she trained herself and her dogs to get ready for the next year. Susan also took a bit of time in September of 1985 to marry David

Iditarod Tidbits

- IDITAROD is the name of a ghost town in Alaska. The word is a native terms which means "distant place."
- In 1974, Mary Shields became the first woman to finish the Iditarod.
- In 1985, Libby Riddles was the first woman to win the Iditarod. Susan Butcher won in 1986, 1987, and 1988. A favorite slogan on the T-shirts of race fans read: ALASKA, WHERE THE MEN ARE MEN AND WOMEN WIN THE IDITAROD.
- Each team averages sixteen dogs. Tired and ill dogs are left at checkpoints along the race to receive care.

Monson, a fellow musher. The following year, 1986, Susan won her first race in record time.

Susan shared the limelight with her dogs. At the finish line, Susan and her lead dogs were draped in flowers. "They're everything," Susan said, "my friends, family, and co-workers. They are the athletes and are trained and chosen for competition just like any athlete." Susan, her dogs, and later, David, trained on a five-acre camp twenty-five miles from the nearest town of Manley, which has a population of less than ninety.

The dog population at the Trail Breaker Kennels is larger than the town's, with numbers reaching up to 150. And Susan knew them all. She could even recognize each dog by its voice. She developed an intense relationship with the dogs as she trained them every day for fourteen to sixteen hours.

Susan Butcher Tidbits

* Susan and David named their first daughter Margaretha Tekla. Tekla was the name of Susan's first lead dog.

* At Susan and David's wedding, the lead dogs, Tekla and Granite, served as ring bearers.

* In 2007, Governor Sarah Palin proclaimed March 3 as Susan Butcher Day, after Susan's death to cancer.

March
3

Susan Butcher chose this life, and she wanted it. She grew up in Cambridge, Massachusetts, but even as a child, she didn't want to be there. In first grade, one of her essays read, "I hate the city." She longed for the outdoors where she could run and play with her dog, Cabee. After high school, Susan left the city for Colorado. She took her first husky dog with her. In Colorado, she and Manganak learned to mush.

Colorado was still too crowded, so Susan left for Alaska when she was twenty. Susan had found her place. It was far away, but she felt at home in the wilderness. For a decade, her cabin had no running water, no telephone, and no electricity. Susan filled her life with friends, dog friends. The dogs were her buddies. She combined her love of the wilderness with her love of dogs by becoming a musher.

After her three consecutive wins in 1986, 1987, and 1988, Susan took second in 1989. Some of her dogs had fallen ill during the race. In 1990, she raced again and won. She became the second person, and the only woman, to win four Iditarod races. But the title of woman musher was not important to Susan. She stated, "I was very aware that I was a woman and that this was a big thing for women, but I didn't want to be given any special treatment. I just wanted to be viewed as a musher." And a musher she was. A musher and a CHAMPION.

↖ Artist Jon Van Zyle's 1988 Iditarod poster, "More than a race . . . a discovery of self."

Mt. EVEREST=
20 EMPIRE
STATE
BUILDINGS

dare
to
fail

kit DesLauriers

confidence

KIT DESLAURIERS
(b.1969)

A reporter from *American Way Magazine* once asked Kit DesLauriers how she kept up with the Women's Freeskiing competitors who were so much younger. There was a long pause. "Well, the record should show that it's not me who is keeping up with them," Kit DesLauriers answered with CONFIDENCE. In 2004 and 2005, Kit was the World Freeskiing Women's Champion.

"Don't let dreams be dreams," believes Kit DesLauriers. In 1995, Kit had a dream of skiing the tallest peak on each continent of the world, the Seven Summits. No one had ever done it. Kit succeeded in being the first.

Did Kit have skills? She made sure she did. Kit DesLauriers is an experienced mountain climber. In 1998, she climbed to the top of a Himalayan mountaintop. "On this trek I was looking all around me and I had this life changing moment," Kit remembers. "All I could think was

← Kit crossing the summit ridge of Mt. Everest.

↙ Alpine skis

23

why didn't I have my skis with me." Kit decided to work on her skiing so that she could ski any mountain.

Was she scared? Sometimes. She admits, "Often enough to be comfortable with it. It's knowing what your limits are." Kit knew being scared would make her careful but being fearful would make her helpless.

Kit only told a handful of people about her personal mission to ski the Seven Summits. She told her husband and invited him to join her. She didn't tell her parents, although they figured it out. DesLauriers didn't want her friends and family to worry. She also knew it was possible she may change her mind. It was her goal and her choice as to whether she completed it or not.

Before her decision, Kit had already skied the highest peak in North America, Denali (or Mount McKinley) located in Alaska. In April 2005, she had six more to go. At Vinson Massif in Antarctica, it was so cold that water thrown into the air would freeze before it hit the ground. But she made it up to the peak with her husband and they skied down.

On October 18, 2006, Kit DesLauriers had only one summit left. Kit stood on

"I've always tried to do whatever my heart has in it, whether it was acceptable or perceived as possible or not."

—Kit DesLauriers

The Seven Summits as Kit Skied Them

Summit	Continent	Elevation in feet	Comparison to Empire State Building
Denali (Mt. McKinley)	North America	20,322	14
Elbrus	Europe	18,510	12¾
Kosciuszko	Australia	7,310	5
Vinson Massif	Antarctica	16,050	11
Aconcagua	South America	22,841	16
Kilimanjaro	Africa	19,340	13
Everest	Asia	29,035	20

Note: The height of the Empire State Building is 1,454 feet, including the television antenna mast.

the top of the world, Mount Everest. To the right was Nepal and a 9,000-foot drop. To the left was China and an 8,000-foot drop. In front of her she saw hard-packed snow and a forty-foot drop. For miles in all directions, mountaintops peeked through the clouds. Kit, Rob, and their friend Jimmy Chin had climbed up, and now it was time to ski down.

Since the air at the top of the world is so thin, time was of the essence. They only had so much oxygen in their bottles. Kit put on her skis, pointed the tips over the edge of the peak, and pushed off. With that push, Kit DesLauriers went down the summit and down into history.

"Skiing off the summit of Everest, I don't know if I ever felt such joy in slipping on my skis and sliding on the snow," Kit said of the moment. After skiing down the distance of about a football field, she stopped. The Hillary Step, a great rock

Kit prepares to rappel the Hillary Step.

"Dare to fail."

—Kit DesLauriers

← Rob and Kit on the Summit
of Mt. Everest.

Also in 2006

* Pluto is downsized from being called a planet.

* Wii is released to the public.

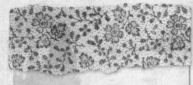

Kit DesLauriers Tidbits

- Kit and Rob had a baby girl on December 16, 2007. They named her Grace.
- Kit DesLauriers strapped on her first pair of downhill skis at age fourteen.

ledge, was not skiable. Too much rock and not enough snow covered the outcropping. Kit took off her skis and climbed down to make camp.

The next day was the greatest ski challenge of Kit's life—skiing down the Lhotse Face, which is nearly a mile of ice steeper than the stairs in a house and steeper than the steepest street in the world. There would be no way to turn back. One mistake and she would be a mangled heap lying at the bottom. At one point Kit skied up to Rob. Her husband asked, "Kit, how are you doing?" Kit replied, "I'm scared. I don't want to die." She coached herself all the way down saying, "Like your life depends on it. Turn!"

At the bottom, she had skied her last summit. Kit could celebrate. She was the first person to ski the highest peak on each continent! Her personal goal had become legendary. The DesLaurierses were swamped with interviews. People admired Kit for her skills, her bravery, her gusto, but mostly her SELF-CONFIDENCE.

On June 16, 1963, Valentina Tereshkova climbed into her bulky space suit. At this time, there were no cell phones, no personal computers, and no colored televisions. The first man had blasted into space only several years before. Valentina's heart pounded as she waited inside her spacecraft, *Vostok 6*, for takeoff. She was about to become the first woman to ascend to the stars. Yes, she was afraid, but Tereshkova was COURAGEOUS.

Valentina practices feeding in simulated flight conditions for her flight as the first woman in space on the VOSTOK 6 mission.

Only two years earlier, the Soviet Union had decided to put a woman into space. Valentina sent in an application. She was not a pilot or an engineer or a scientist. She worked on a loom in a textile factory in the small town where she had grown up. She did know how to parachute; it was her hobby. And she wanted to go to space.

"Once you are at this faraway distance, you realize the significance of what it is that unites us. Let us work together to overcome our differences."

—Valentina Tereshkova

Three, two, one. Launch! Valentina heard a thunderous roar. The rocket shook and shivered. The cosmonaut said to herself, "I'm flying." Her hands and feet felt heavy. She couldn't even move a finger. The pressure grew as she tore through the gravity of Earth.

Valentina prepared for this flight for eighteen months in the "Star City." The women applicants were narrowed from fifty-eight to five. Valentina was the only one without a higher education. These five women spent each day running treadmills, enduring heat chambers, spinning in flight simulators, being alone in isolation chambers, training to be pilots, and parachute jumping. They met the male cosmonauts who had been in space or would soon be. They met the scientists and engineers responsible for getting them safely into space and back home again. They also attended lectures to learn about space and aeronautics.

Even with all the preparation, Tereshkova could not collect her

Women Today

* Less than one in eight women work in science or engineering.

thoughts as she hurdled to the heavens. A voice surprised her. She shook her head. It was the voice of the first man in space. It came from the command center telling her everything was excellent and the machine was working great. The great pressure eased, and she could breathe again.

There could only be one "first woman in space." Valentina was chosen for what she could do. She excelled in her physical training.

Valentina was also chosen for what she could not do. She was not a trained pilot. They saved several of the trained women for later flights, which might need pilot skills. Tereshkova's flight would be autopiloted, like all the previous space flights had been.

Valentina was modest and very patriotic. One of the other candidates was excluded because her behavior was considered unacceptable. She

Valentina exercising, January 10, 1963 ⟶

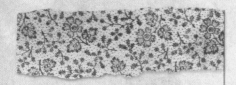

Valentina Tereshkova Tidbits

- In November of 1963, Tereshkova and a fellow cosmonaut, Andrian Nikolayev, married. They had a daughter.
- A crater on the far side of the moon was named after her.
- Valentina was a torch-bearer in the 2008 Summer Olympics torch relay in St. Petersburg, Russia.

Also in 1963

* President John F. Kennedy is assassinated.

* The Beatles song "I Want to Hold Your Hand" becomes their first hit.

expressed her views that decent women could smoke cigarettes, and she left the compound to visit town without a chaperone.

Valentina was intelligent, but she was not educated. People could identify with their new hero.

Valentina viewed the world as no woman had ever seen it before, from space. She peered out the porthole and spoke into the radio, "I am Chaika. I see the horizon. There is a blue stripe. This is the Earth. How beautiful it is! Everything is going well." Chaika, her radio call name, means "seagull" in Russian. And she flew high above the Earth.

The cosmonaut remained strapped to her seat for almost three days, except for a brief time. But no one heard her complain. She barely ate, as the food made her sick, and she developed a leg cramp and a rash on

← Pilot Cosmonaut Valentina Nikolaeva Tereshkova wearing medals, November 21, 1963

her shoulder. But the public never knew. She would orbit Earth forty-eight times. Women from all over the world felt proud to have a woman in space.

As Valentina flew over the area where she grew up, she strained to see her city, "the soul was anxious to fly back to our native planet, to the friends and close people." Much of the world was listening when she spoke into her radio. "Tell Mama not to worry," the COURAGEOUS first woman into space assured her mother and the world.

After three days, Tereshkova safely arrived back on Earth. It would be twenty years before the next woman, Sally Ride, would enter space.

"All adventures, especially into new territory, are scary."

—Sally Ride, first American woman in space

Bessie Coleman

DETERMINATION

If **I** CAN create the minimum of my plans and desires, there shall be NO regrets.

BESSIE COLEMAN
(1892–1926)

Bessie stands on the wheel of a plane. ⤴

Bessie Coleman flew above the crowd. From the open cockpit of her plane, she saw the gathered folks of Waxahachie, Texas. She knew many of them. This was her hometown. She insisted the audience be desegregated so that her people could see the show. The people looked up at her flying high in the sky! She had left Waxahachie only ten short years ago in 1915. Now she was no longer the daughter of sharecroppers. She was no longer a maid in the white people's houses. She was Queen Bess, the first licensed black aviator in the world. Many people looked up to her for her courage and DETERMINATION.

Bessie Coleman's portrait that was later used by the US Postal Service in 1995 to commemorate a Black Heritage stamp.

Bessie refused to accept a common life. She always knew she wanted something better, something more than what most African Americans in the early 1900s would expect. This was a time when black and white people in the United States

"Flying does not rely so much on strength, as on physical and mental coordination."

—Elise Deroche, first woman to fly an airplane solo

Bessie Coleman in uniform.

were kept separate by law. They went to separate schools and lived in separate

neighborhoods. Black people even went to separate movie houses or had to wait for the midnight film showing, when the white people were gone from the theater.

Bessie was black and a woman. Women did not yet have the right to vote in the United States. A popular English novelist of the times, Arnold Bennett, wrote in his book *Our Women*, "And the truth is that intellectually and creatively man is superior of woman . . ." Bessie wouldn't let being a black woman stop her from what she wanted to do, fly an airplane.

Bessie read about the Wright brothers and Harriet Quimby, the first American woman to fly. While working in a barbershop as a manicurist, Bessie heard soldiers returning from World War I say that in France women could fly planes. Bessie later recalled, "All the articles I read finally convinced me I should be up there flying and not just reading about it."

Bessie tried to find a flight school to teach her. However, even African American men were not allowed to train as pilots during WWI. There were no flight schools for black people since there were no black pilots to serve as

Bessie Coleman Tidbits

- A stamp honoring Bessie Coleman was released in 1995.
- On April 30, the date of Coleman's death, African American men and women pilots fly over the Lincoln Cemetery in Chicago and drop flowers upon her grave.

trainers. Bessie was determined. She asked advice from her friend Robert Abbott, the publisher of the black newspaper, the *Chicago Defender.* He told her to go to France, where race would not be such an issue.

In 1920, Bessie set sail. She enrolled in one of the best aviation schools in France. Bessie signed a contract stating the flight school was not responsible for her life. During her training, a fellow student died. She said, "I saw a pupil killed instantly; it was a terrible shock to my nerves, but I never lost them. I kept on going."

In 1921, Bessie Coleman returned to the United States as the first black person to earn a pilot's license. Many black newspapers and several white

THE CHICAGO DEFENDER, *October 8, 1921*

THE CHICAGO DEFENDER, May 8, 1926,
Article by E.B. Jourdain, Jr.

Aero Club de France pilot license issued
June 15, 1921, in France to Mlle. Bessie Coleman.

Federation Aeronautique Internationale
FRANCE

Nous soussignés pouvoir sportif reconnu par la Federation Aeronautique Internationale pour la France certifions que

Mme *Bessie Coleman* née a *Atlanta, Texas* le *20 Janvier 1896* ayant rempli toutes les conditions composées par la F.A.I. a été breveté

Pilote–Aviateur

a la date du *15 Juin 1921*

Signature du Titulaire
Bessie Coleman

N. du Brevet *18.310*

newspapers interviewed her. Even with the publicity, Coleman couldn't put her license to use.

US airmail had started, but the job was reserved for white males only. There were no commercial passenger airlines. But there were barnstormers. These were stunt pilots who performed daring feats for paying crowds. After more training in Europe, Bessie became a barnstormer.

Bessie went on the road to perform aerial shows. She was female. She was black. She could fly a plane. She was a novelty. She was "Queen Bess," "Brownskin Bess," and "Brave Bessie."

Bessie used her celebrity status well. She saw flying as a future for African Americans. Her goal was to open a black aviation school. Bessie lectured to crowds in black churches and meeting halls. She was motivational—not just with her words, but with her actions.

Also in 1921

* The first highway designed for cars, the Autobahn, opens for traffic in Berlin, Germany.

* The first radio broadcast of a baseball game is of the Pittsburgh Pirates vs. the Philadelphia Phillies.

Bessie insisted that African Americans be allowed into her air shows. One time she held up a show in Orlando, Florida, until pamphlets were distributed in the black community inviting them to attend. She thrilled the mixed crowds with figure eights, barrel rolls, and loop-the-loops.

One day, Bessie bought her own plane. It was an old one. Nearly 10,000 people gathered on February 4, 1923, for her first show in California. But Bessie never arrived. Her plane crashed on the way to the show. Bessie broke her leg and several ribs. She sent a telegram saying, "Tell them all that as soon as I can walk, I'm going to fly." It was almost two years before Bessie was back in the air.

Women Today

* In the 1920s only six percent of licensed pilots were female. Today the percentage is still the same. Less than one percent are African American women.

On April 30, 1926, Bessie and her mechanic, William D. Wills, climbed into her new plane. Bessie was preparing for her benefit performance at the May Day celebration of the Negro Welfare League in Jacksonville, Florida. About ten minutes after takeoff, the plane went into a spin. Brave Bessie was hurled from the plane and plunged five hundred feet to her death. Her plane crashed to the ground nearby.

Thousands of people attended her memorial services. They came to honor not just the first black aviator, but the woman who embodied fearlessness and DETERMINATION.

EXTRAORDINARY

LADY
and GENTLEMEN,
START YOUR ENGINES!

JANET
GUTHRIE

68

Janet Guthrie
(b. 1938)

anet Guthrie sat behind the wheel of her souped-up Lightning car. No, she wasn't just a pretty face selling the car at an Auto Show. She was a race-car driver in the Indianapolis 500, the "Greatest Spectacle in Racing." It was 1977 and Janet Guthrie would be the first woman to race the Indy 500.

Before 1971, for sixty years since the race began, women were not even allowed on the track, in the pit, in the garages, or in the press box but for one exception in 1956. Before 1971, women could own race cars but getting near the racetrack was forbidden. Before 1971, women were only seen on the track after the race was

⤺ Janet Guthrie becomes the first woman to finish the Indianapolis 500 in 1977.

⤺ Janet is all smiles as her pit crew swarms around her following the Indy 500-Mile Race in Indianapolis, IN, Sunday, May 28, 1978.

⟵ Janet at the track in Concord, NC, before the World 600 auto race in May 1976.

over, beauties in the winner's circle, kissing and posing with the male drivers.

All of that changed with Janet Guthrie, the

EXTRAORDINARY first lady of racing.

45

"**Not everyone wants to drive race cars, but for each person, the right challenge is out there, the challenge that is just the right size, the challenge that will evoke the best that a person can be.**"

—Janet Guthrie,

from *Janet Guthrie: A Life at Full Throttle*

"Gentlemen, start your engines!" was the traditional call to begin the race, but now there was a female racer. Quite the dilemma. The racetrack owner said he would still shout the traditional opening because the mechanics actually started the cars. However, Kay Bignotti, a mechanic and daughter of a three-time Indianapolis 500 winner, offered to start Janet's engine.

In 1977, the command was "In company with the first woman ever to qualify at Indianapolis, gentlemen, start your engines." Guthrie later said, "Well, frankly, I couldn't have cared less what they said as long as mine was one of the engines that started."

And start her engine she did. Each year only thirty-three cars compete in this prestigious race. To even get to the starting line, you have to qualify by driving as fast as you can for ten miles, or four laps on the oval track. Janet had tried in 1976, but she didn't make the necessary time. Then, in 1977, she nailed a position with a speed of 188.4 miles per hour. She was fast—the fastest car of that qualifying weekend. Guthrie was in the race.

Now, instead of four laps, Janet had two hundred laps to go. The 500 in "Indianapolis 500" refers to the number of miles. Racers must withstand high-speed racing for five to seven hours. "There is very little in civilized life that demands everything you got intellectually, physically, and emotionally. Driving is living. It's aggressive instead of passive living," asserts Janet. One slip of the body or the mind and you could crash. Janet knew this.

Janet poses with a toy race car at a news conference in New York City, Thursday, April 6, 1978. Texaco announced its plans to provide financing for Guthrie's Texaco Star and supporting pit crew that would permit her to compete in the 1978 Indy 500 Memorial Day weekend.

Women Racers in the Indianapolis 500

Racer	Years Raced in the Indy 500
Janet Guthrie	1977, 1978, 1979
Lyn St. James	1992, 1993, 1994, 1995, 1996, 1997, 2000
Sarah Fisher	2000, 2001, 2002, 2003, 2004, 2007, 2008, 2009, 2010
Danica Patrick	2005, 2006, 2007, 2008, 2009, 2010, 2011
Milka Duno	2007, 2008, 2009
Ana Beatriz	2010, 2011
Simona de Silvestro	2010, 2011
Pippa Mann	2011

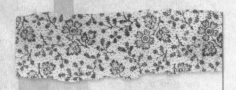

Janet Guthrie Tidbits

- She was inducted into the International Motorsports Hall of Fame in 2006.
- Janet wrote a book about her life titled JANET GUTHRIE: A LIFE AT FULL THROTTLE.
- Before her racing career, Guthrie was a physicist working in aviation.

Also in 1977

* The movie STAR WARS is released.

* Elvis Presley dies.

Race day arrived. The air swirled around her helmet. As she sped around the track, the world looked like it was underwater. The Lightning squeaked by another car with inches to spare. On the fifteenth lap, her engine snapped and crackled. She pulled into the pit but refused to get out of the car. As she waited, an overflow valve opened, spilling fuel down Janet's back and covering the seat. Janet stayed put in her car ready to return to the race. The crew poured water over her. And she was off!

Janet drove for almost two hours soaked in fuel. The engine problems finally forced her to stop. For Janet the race was over. Guthrie finished in twenty-ninth place. The crowd in the pit-side grandstands gave her a standing ovation as she walked off the racetrack. She waved and called out, "Next year." Janet headed for the only shower to wash off her fuel-soaked body. The shower was in the men's bathroom.

"Lady and gentlemen, start your engines!" As promised, Janet was back in 1978. This time she was in a different car, the Wildcat. And this time, Janet was more in control. She had formed her team, and she managed it herself. Everything was going great until two days before the race, when Guthrie fractured her wrist while she was playing tennis at a fundraising event. However, a broken wrist was not about to stop her. On race day, Janet climbed into her car and waved to her parents. "And from then on, nothing existed but the track and the cars and the signals from my crew," remembers Guthrie.

After hours of driving, her wrist was painful. But she only had one lap left. Guthrie saw the checkered flag at the finish line, and she floored it. Janet finished the race and in ninth place! **EXTRAORDINARY!**

Janet Guthrie, #68, stands in front of her car before the 1977 Winston Cup Daytona 500 on February 20, 1977, at the Daytona International Speedway in Daytona Beach, FL.

Adventure is Worthwhile in itself.

Amelia Earhart

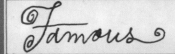

Famous

AMELIA EARHART
(b.1897, missing 1937)

A melia Earhart, the famous aviator, was ready to do it for real this time. She would fly across the Atlantic Ocean. Four years earlier she was celebrated worldwide for being the first woman to fly across the Atlantic Ocean. But for Amelia it wasn't a real flight since she had not flown the plane. The pilot was Bill Stultz. Amelia never even touched the controls. Her job was to keep the flight log, and she did not think that was flying.

When Amelia agreed to be the first woman to cross the Atlantic in a plane, she knew she wouldn't be at the controls, even though she could fly. Amelia was a licensed pilot, and she owned

↖ Portrait of aviatrix Amelia Earhart, 1932

her own bright yellow plane. The wealthy woman sponsoring the flight,

← A crowd cheers for aviatrix Amelia Earhart as she boards her single-engine Lockheed Vega airplane in Londonderry, Northern Ireland, for the trip back to London on May 22, 1932.

Amy Guest, wanted the "right sort of girl" and that girl had to be American. The

project coordinators interviewed Amelia Earhart. She was attractive, bright, and

confident. Also, Earhart looked like a female version of Charles Lindbergh, the

first person to fly alone across the Atlantic Ocean. Amelia fit the bill.

Amelia boarded the airplane in Boston Harbor as an unknown person. By the

time she touched down on June 19, 1928, in the sea off of Wales, she was

FAMOUS. Even with all of the fame, Amelia was not satisfied with herself. She

knew she could pilot the flight. On May 20, 1932, exactly five years after

Amelia Earhart Tidbits

- After a dinner party with President Roosevelt and Eleanor Roosevelt, Amelia slipped out with the First Lady to go flying. They were both wearing evening gowns.
- Earhart was a part of the public eye. She designed a women's clothing line for "active living" and had luggage named after her, Modernaire Earhart Luggage.

↰ Amelia Earhart, June 4, 1928

"Adventure is worthwhile in itself."

—Amelia Earhart

Amelia waves from the Electra before taking → off from Los Angeles, CA, on March 10, 1937. Earhart was flying to Oakland, CA, where she and her crew would begin their round-the-world flight to Howland Island on March 18.

Lindbergh's flight, Earhart took off from Newfoundland, Canada, on her quest to become the first woman to fly a plane across the Atlantic.

Amelia carried a flying suit, thermos of soup, and can of tomato juice with a straw. Her first few hours went smoothly. Then her altimeter failed. Unless there was light, Amelia couldn't tell how far above the waves she was flying. As clouds blocked the moonlight, Earhart knew things were about to get worse. She flew right into a storm. Amelia flew higher to get above the clouds, but ice formed on the wings.

THE WHITE HOUSE
WASHINGTON

January 18, 1935

My dear Miss Earhart:

I am pleased to send you this message of congratulations. You have scored again.

By successfully spanning the ocean stretches between Hawaii and California, following your triumphant trans-Atlantic flight of 1928, you have shown even the "doubting Thomases" that aviation is a science which cannot be limited to men only.

Because of swift advances in this science of flight, made possible by Government and private enterprise, scheduled ocean transportation by air is a distinct and definite future prospect.

The trail-blazers who opened to civilization the vast stretches of this Continent of ours, who moved our boundary from the Atlantic to the Pacific, were inspired and helped by women of courage and skill. From the days of these pioneers to the present era, women have marched step in step with men. And now, when air trails between our shores and those of our neighbors are being charted, you, as a woman, have preserved and carried forward this precious tradition.

Very sincerely yours,

Franklin D Roosevelt

Miss Amelia Earhart,
Oakland, California.

Amelia Earhart, ca. 1935

Letter from President Franklin Roosevelt to
Amelia Earhart, January 18, 1935.

Amelia recalled, "I descended to hunt for warmer air to melt the ice. Down I went until I could see the whitecaps through the fog. It was unpleasant there, because sudden heavy fog and a dip would land me in the ocean. So I climbed until the ice began to form again. Then down again to the fog above the waves." Flames shot out from her exhaust pipe where a crack had formed. Amelia continued to yo-yo over the ocean keeping her eyes on the flames trailing behind the plane.

Daylight arrived. Her fuel gauge leaked, sending fumes into the cockpit. Amelia knew she had to land right away. She spotted green—land.

"Of course, I came down in a pasture and I had to circle many other pastures to find the best one. The horses, sheep, and cows in Londonderry were not used to airplanes, and so, as I flew low, they jumped up and down and displayed certain disquiet." She landed safely in a field in Ireland to become the first

Also in 1932

* Fritos corn chips sell for the first time.

* Shirley Temple makes her first film.

"The most effective way to do it, is to do it."

—Amelia Earhart

woman to fly across the Atlantic. And she did it solo. Again she would return to the United States a hero, but this time she felt good about it.

Five years later, Amelia was prepared to make history again. She planned to become the first woman to fly around the world. She would follow the equator, a route no pilot had ever tried. First she tried by leaving from California and heading west. But this attempt ended early when she crashed taking off from Hawaii. Amelia was still determined to go. So she planned a second flight, this time traveling east from California. Before the flight, Amelia told a reporter, "I won't feel completely cheated if I fail to come back."

On May 21, 1937, the plane took off. Amelia was the pilot, and her friend Fred Noonan was the navigator. After six weeks, they had covered twenty-two thousand miles! They had flown through storms, seen jungles, and slept in deserts. Only 2,556 miles to go! For the last leg of the trip, Amelia would fly from New Guinea over the Pacific to a tiny island called Howland. It was so small, it would be difficult to find. A coast guard ship, the *Itasca*, would help to guide her. Then she would jump from Howland Island to Hawaii and home to California.

On July 2, 1937, Amelia and Fred took off for Howland Island. But they never made it to the island. And they never made it home. After takeoff, no one saw the FAMOUS aviator Amelia Earhart ever again.

Amelia and her navigator, Fred Noonan, pose in front of their twin-engine Lockheed Electra in Los Angeles at the end of May 1937, prior to their flight around the world.

Front page of THE EVENING SUN, July 3, 1937. →

Intrepid

Sophie BLANCHARD

ON the wings of the stiffening morning breeze we raced along in joyous flight like a happy swallow...
contessa Grace di Campello Della Spin
hot air balloon hobbrist

O n the evening of July 6, 1819, Sophie Blanchard "the **INTREPID** little flyer" climbed into her small basket. Her silk balloon billowed large over her head. Several thousand people gathered at Tivoli Gardens in Paris, France, to see her famous display. Sparklers twinkled from her balloon floating in the sky. She dropped small parachutes carrying burning pots that exploded and danced in the air. Some people said it was too dangerous for her to set off fireworks from her

An engraving of Marie Madeleine Sophie Armant from the book ALBUM OF SCIENCE FAMOUS SCIENTIST DISCOVERIES in 1899

place in the sky. But the balloonist performed as often as twice a week. She lived for her flights. It was the only place where she felt calm and free.

Sophie's balloon was lighter than air. It was not a hot air balloon but a hydrogen balloon. Hydrogen gas

← A Print of Jean Pierre Blanchard (Sophie's future husband) and John Jeffries arriving in Calais after crossing the English Channel in a hot air balloon, 1785.

is lighter than air and very flammable. Once the silk orb filled with the gas, she didn't have to do a thing. Tonight, however, a strong wind blew. As the balloon struggled to rise, it brushed against some tree branches. Once clear of the trees and above the crowd, Sophie waved her white flag to signal that the show was about to begin.

Sophie grew up in a hamlet near the coast of France. She never saw a balloon until she married Jean-Pierre Blanchard, a famous French balloonist. He took Sophie up in a balloon following their marriage in 1804. After two flights with Jean-Pierre, she wanted to fly alone. Sophie Blanchard became the first female balloonist to fly solo. On land, Sophie was very nervous. Sudden noises and carriage rides terrified her. But up in the air

French Balloonmania

During the 1780s, French fashion and home decor were "au balloon." Balloons were painted on plates, teapots, gloves, vests, fans, and wallpaper. Stylish people wore balloon hats. The first toy balloons also appeared.

From
IT'S ELECTRIC TIMES
SOPHIE BLANCHARD

Were you as scared, afright as they
    said you were?
Afraid of the
warnings that day, that flame and
    fire, the cross
of ancient and modern, or sacred and
    baleful,
would overwhelm you and your basket?
The winds, they blew you off course,
    but
it was no matter for your ballooning
    expertise,
my love.
You who feared cannon-shot, who
    feared the
click-clack, click-clack of
    horse-hoofs or the
rolling thunder of a passenger
    carriage,
You my sweet tremble, soft and
    nervous
like a bird,
you broke free, ascending into the
    night sky
like a bubble drifting ever higher
    into ethereal darkness,
But you did not notice the trees had
    dislodged
your fireworks, and it was to be
    your end.
                    —Hilton Hightower, 2007

she had an "incomparable sensation." Sophie was "small with bird-like features." And she took to the air like she was born there.

Soon, like her husband, she was performing. When her husband died in 1809, Sophie continued to grace the skies. She rose above French cities, countryside, and politics. Emperor Napoleon was so taken by Madame Blanchard's performance he made her "Aeronaut of the Official Festivals." For the celebration of Napoleon's marriage to Marie Louise, she ascended in a balloon decorated with eagles, greenery, and a female figure. When Napoleon's son was born, Sophie floated over the streets of Paris dropping birth announce-ments upon the people below.

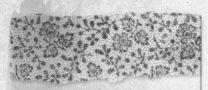

Sophie Blanchard Tidbits

- Sophie went up in her balloon 67 times.
- Sophie Blanchard's tombstone is engraved with "victim of her art and intrepidity."

Napoleon was exiled in 1813, but that didn't stop Madame Blanchard. When King Louis XVIII returned to the throne, he was so impressed by the woman balloonist, she became the "Official Aeronaut of the Restoration."

In her balloon, Sophie was fearless. On a flight out of Rome, she rose so high that she suffered the extremes of heat and cold. She fell into a deep sleep, during which her balloon reached 12,000 feet. To avoid a hailstorm on another flight, Blanchard again attained heights so great that she passed out. She crossed the Alps by balloon where the temperature dropped so low that icicles formed on her hands and feet. She almost drowned on her fifty-third flight after her balloon caught in a tree and she fell into water. Still Sophie flew. And nighttime was her favorite.

On that windy July night at Tivoli Gardens, Sophie put down her white flag

Also in 1819

- The first chocolate factory opens in Switzerland.
- In England, children are no longer allowed to work for more than twelve hours a day.

SOPHIE BLANCHARD

M. S. BLANCHARD celebre aeronauta
il cimento del volo aerostatico da lei eseguito in Milano
in presenza delle LL. A. A. II. e R. R.
la sera del 22 Agosto 1811

← Full-length portrait of Sophie standing in the decorated basket of her balloon during her flight in Milan, Italy, in 1811, in the presence of the imperial and royal highness.

and began her show. As Sophie's balloon passed through clouds, the spectators' view was blurred. The crowd cheered as Madame Blanchard's balloon came back into clear view—in flames! The cheers turned to screams as the balloon fell from the sky. The wind pushed the balloon over the city. Sophie wrung her hands in despair.

"Then, with the fortune of those talented in their calling, you managed to steer your basket onto a rooftop, and for a moment your heart soared that you just might make it, but the pitch was too much, and you were cast headlong over the roof and into the proud street below."

— From *It's Electric Times Sophie Blanchard*, by Hilton Hightower, 2007

↖ Engraving depicts Sophie's death on July 6, 1819, in the Rue de Provence Paris from the book ALBUM OF SCIENCE FAMOUS SCIENTIST DISCOVERIES in 1899.

The INTREPID balloonist, Sophie Blanchard, would forever be remembered for her courage and her artistry.

NORTHERN HEMISPHERE.

NELLiE BLY MAVerick

If we want good work from others or wish to accomplish anything ourselves, it will never do to harbor a **doubt** as to the result of an enterprise.

PRESENTING THE GLOBE-GIRDLER A GOLDEN GLOBE.

THE ARRIVAL IN PHILADELPHIA.

AROUND THE WORLD IN SEVENTY-TWO DAYS AND SIX HOURS—RECEPTION OF NELLIE BLY AT JERSEY CITY ON THE COM
OF HER JOURNEY.—From Sketches by C. Bunnell.—[See Page 1.]

Nellie Bly
(1864–1922)

Nellie Bly was a newspaper reporter. You may be thinking, "There are lots of newspaper women. What's the big deal?" But Nellie Bly was a newspaper reporter in the late 1800s. In those days, the few women who wrote for the paper only covered topics like cooking, fashion, and parties. Nellie Bly was one of the first journalists to do investigative work. She was on the front lines of reporting. She refused to hold to the stereotype for a woman of her time. If it were not for Nellie Bly, women today might still be reporting solely on hairstyles and the best recipe for apple crisp. Nellie Bly was a MAVERICK.

Nellie Bly's whole career started because she felt offended and she did something about it. Nellie was not yet known as Nellie

Portrait of Nellie Bly

← Newspaper article on Nellie, depicting her reception in Jersey City upon completion of her journey.

> "To love what you do and feel that it matters—how could anything be more fun?"
>
> —Katharine Graham, publisher of the WASHINGTON POST

Nellie Bly Tidbit

Her family called her Pink because as a child her mother dressed her in pink dresses with white stockings. In the mid-1800s little girls didn't wear pink like today. They wore gray or brown dresses with black stockings.

Bly. Her name was Elizabeth Jane Cochran, but her family called her Pink.

Pink read a column in a January 1885 *Pittsburg Dispatch* titled "What Girls Are Good For?" The columnist wrote that in some countries people got rid of baby girls because there was no good use for them. Pink wrote a letter telling of her plight. She could not find a decent job just because she was a woman. She signed the letter "Lonely Orphan Girl" because her family was left poor after the death of her father. She sent the letter with no return address.

Her letter never saw print. Instead,

these words appeared in the *Pittsburg Dispatch*: "If the writer of the communication signed 'Lonely Orphan Girl' will send her name and address to this office . . ." Pink didn't send her name and address—she showed right up.

Pink was asked to write a response piece to the column she read. She did. The piece was titled, "The Girl Puzzle." It was not considered proper for a woman to write under her real name. The editor chose Pink's pen name, Nellie Bly. So the world would not know her as Pink, or as Elizabeth Cochran, but as Nellie Bly.

Less than one year later, Nellie found herself a resident of an insane asylum in New York. No, she was not crazy; she was undercover. Nellie faked being insane so she would be committed. She wanted to learn the truth about how patients were treated and she got it.

Also in 1890

* POEMS by Emily Dickinson is published.

* Peanut butter is invented.

VIEW OF THE LUNATIC ASYLUM AND MAD HOUSE, ON BLACKWELL'S ISLAND, NEW YORK.

The lunatic asylum and mad house, on Blackwell's Island, NY, 1853.

Copyright 1890 by H. J. Myers.

Myers

Nellie Bly

No. 7

1399 Broadway N. Y.

6326

"If we want good work from others or wish to
accomplish anything ourselves, it will never do to
harbor a doubt as to the result of an enterprise."

—Nellie Bly

Printed on the same page as Nelly Bly's story, "Ten Days in a Mad-House" was an ad for corsets.

A corset was a combination girdle and bra that squeezed the chest from under the breasts all the way to the stomach. The lovely device was stiffened with slats of wood, whale bone, or leather. Corset fashion got so crazy that in the mid-1800s women pinched their corsets so tight some died from the strain.

WEINGARTEN BROS.

AMERICA'S Leading *Erect Form* & *La Vida* CORSETS

America's leading corset the Erect Form "follows the natural outlines of the form and does not compress the figure into a graceless illogical shape." From THE LADIES FIELD, June 1902.

Nellie wrote, "What, excepting torture, would produce insanity quicker than this treatment? . . . Take a perfectly sane and healthy woman, shut her up and make her sit from 6 am until 8 pm on straight-back benches, do not allow her to talk or move during these hours, give her no reading and let her know nothing of

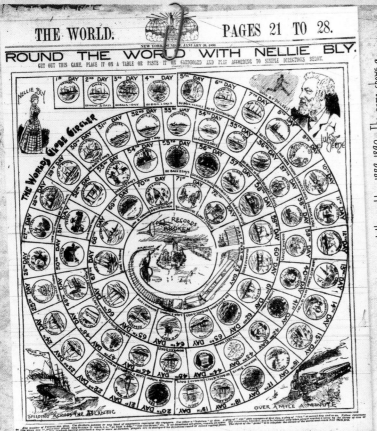

THE WORLD.   PAGES 21 TO 28.

ROUND THE WORLD WITH NELLIE BLY.

CUT OUT THIS GAME, PLACE IT ON A TABLE OR PASTE IT ON CARDBOARD AND PLAY ACCORDING TO SIMPLE DIRECTIONS BELOW.

Board game about Nellie's trip around the world in 1889–1890. The game shows a square for each of the 73 days of her journey arranged in a circular pattern, flanked with images of Bly, Jules Verne, a steam ship and a train. Illustration published in THE WORLD. January 26, 1890.

Around the World in Eighty Days

Jules Verne published a very popular book in 1873 called AROUND THE WORLD IN EIGHTY DAYS. The adventures of Phileas Fogg were told as he circled the globe in what was thought to be amazing speed. Bly set out to break the record of that fictional hero.

the world or its doings, give her bad food and harsh treatment, and see how long it will take to make her insane." Nellie Bly's story "Ten Days in a Mad-House" resulted in an investigation of the institution. Changes were made. Her words made a difference, and Nellie developed a following.

In January of 1890, Nellie Bly got off the train in Jersey City. Thousands of people cheered her name. Cannons boomed out to spread the news of her arrival. Nellie Bly had done it. She had traveled around the world in seventy-two days, six hours, and eleven minutes. Five days less than anyone thought was possible.

And the feat was done by a woman no less! In 1890, women in the United States couldn't enter through the front doors of most hotels, would not think of wearing pants, and did not travel without a chaperone. Now a woman had traveled the entire globe alone and in record time. The mayor of Jersey City said, "The American Girl will no longer be misunderstood. She will be recognized as pushing and determined, independent, able to take care of herself wherever she may go."

Just five years earlier, Lonely Orphan Girl couldn't get a decent job. Now she was the center of attention. Five years ago, Pink had written a letter. Now she wrote stories the entire country read. Nellie Bly was a woman who didn't let the beliefs of her time hold her back. She was a MAVERICK.

A BURNING PURPOSE ATTRACTS OTHERS WHO ARE DRAWN ALONG WITH IT AND HELP FULFILL IT.

RELENTLESS

MARGARET BOURKE-WHITE

Margaret Bourke-White
(1904-1971)

Her photos of factories and steel mills were famous. Headlines read "This Daring Camera Girl Scales Skyscrapers for Art." She lived in a penthouse apartment in New York City. What more could a woman in a man's field of work want?

Margaret Bourke-White had fought to overcome the gender gap. She was an accomplished photographer of skyscrapers, factories, and large construction projects.

In 1934, a dream changed Margaret's life.

← Margaret Bourke-White holding her camera out in field on a farm, July 1946.

Bourke-White had just returned to the New York advertising world after spending five days photographing the Dust Bowl. This assignment was different from taking pictures of buildings. Through the camera's eye she photographed

← Margaret Bourke-White perches on an eagle head gargoyle at the top of the Chrysler Building and focuses a camera. New York, 1935.

"endless dun-colored acres, which should have been green with crops . . ."

"A burning purpose attracts others who are drawn along with it and help fulfill it."

— Margaret Bourke-White, from *Portrait of Myself*

Through her own eyes, she saw "faces engraved with the very paralysis of despair." Times were already hard during the Great Depression, and the lack of rain made it impossible for the farmers to earn a living.

In the 1930s, there were no televisions or computers. People learned about the world by listening to

↖ Margaret prepares to take a picture from high atop a building, New York City, 1931.

Margaret's photograph of farmer Art Blooding with his wife and 4 kids, battling dust bowl 50-mile wind while inspecting his newly bought farm, ⟶ Colorado, 1954.

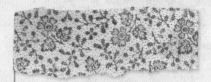

the radio, looking at pictures, and reading newspapers or magazines. Photographers were the eyes of the world.

Back in her fancy New York penthouse, Margaret dreamed the brand new cars from her advertisements were trying to swallow her. She fell out of bed trying to escape the cars. Once awake, she made a promise "that from then on, for the rest of my life, I would undertake only those photographic assignments which I felt could be done in a creative and constructive way." She dropped all of her commercial projects. Margaret Bourke-White began to tell stories with her pictures—the story of people's lives. In this quest, Bourke-White was RELENTLESS.

After her dream, Margaret returned to the South. This time she went with a writer, Erskine Caldwell. They met with the country people in their homes and on their land. Erskine wrote their stories. Margaret captured their worry-worn faces and their bleak lives on her film.

Margaret Bourke-White Tidbits

- At Cornell University, Margaret studied zoology, or the study of animals. When she couldn't find a job on campus, she started taking and selling pictures of the campus.

- After WWII, Margaret Bourke-White continued to photograph injustice throughout the world until she could no longer hold a camera due to Parkinson's disease.

Margaret captured the gaunt, hollow-eyed faces of concentration camp survivors as they gripped the barbed wire fence and stared in wonderment during their liberation from the cruelties of Buchenwald by American forces, April 13, 1945.

In 1937, the words and photos came together in a book, *You Have Seen Their Faces*. Margaret said of the book, "Already it was reaching out, influencing others, and soon was to influence United States legislation, a source of quiet pride to both of us."

World War II, arguably the deadliest conflict in human history, changed everything for Margaret once again. The United States entered the war at the end of 1941. Margaret Bourke-White entered the war in 1942 as the first woman war photographer. She was chosen because her determination to get a photo knew no bounds. And during the war, this would prove true more than ever.

Her assignment was to take photographs for the United States Air Force and for *Life* magazine. Margaret begged to be allowed to fly with the fighter pilots on a bombing mission. She wanted to be in the sky, to be with the action. But those in command thought it was too dangerous for a woman. They even thought it was too dangerous for Bourke-White to fly from Italy to North Africa, so they put her on a ship.

The ship was torpedoed. Everyone had to flee in lifeboats. Bourke-White grabbed one camera and left with the clothes on her back. The rest went down with the ship. After the sinking of the ship, the commanders decided it was okay for the woman photographer to fly on a bomber mission. And she did.

After Germany surrendered in 1945, Bourke-White stayed on to document the defeated country. With the Third Army, she walked into the Buchenwald concentration camp. They were accompanied by two thousand German civilians ordered by the US Army to witness what the Nazis had done. The rumors of the death camps turned into horrific truths. Bourke-White said she worked "with a veil over my mind. In photographing the murder camps, the protective veil was so tightly drawn that I hardly knew what I had taken until I saw prints of my own photographs." Her photographs would stun the world.

As she documented the horror, Margaret kept a family secret to herself, her father was Jewish. "Difficult as these things may be to report or to photograph, it is something we war correspondents must do," she stated. Margaret Bourke-White was RELENTLESS in revealing the truth to the world through the eyes of her camera.

Also in 1934

* The Washeteria opens. It is the first laundromat.

* Gangsters Bonnie and Clyde's lives of crime end.

STRENGTH

GERTRUDE EDERLE

I KNEW if it COULD BE DONE... & I DID it.

GERTRUDE EDERLE
(1906–2003)

Gertrude Ederle had been in the frigid water swimming for twelve hours when the winds whipped up. Her trainer asked her if she was ready to be pulled out. Trudy replied, "Don't stop me. Don't touch me. I'm doing this." She swam on. Gertrude's coach demanded the nineteen-year-old girl be removed. He was stopped by Mr. Ederle, who repeated his daughter's final words before she got into the sea, "Don't let anyone take me out of the water unless I ask." Gertrude swam on.

Gertrude Ederle at the beach, Long Island, NY, 1923.

Have you ever run the 100-yard dash? Now imagine running that distance 370 times. Have you ever swum the length of an Olympic-sized swimming pool? Now imagine doing it 676 times. What would it take for you to complete such a feat?

It would take perseverance. Gertrude Ederle had perseverance. It would take strength. Gertrude Ederle had STRENGTH.

Gertrude enters the turbulent waters off the English Channel, for the start of her record-breaking swim across to the Chalk Cliffs, Dover, England, August 6, 1926.

Gertrude becomes the first woman to swim the English Channel on August 6, 1926, as she crosses the waterway in 14 hours and 31 minutes.

IRELAND

ENGLAND

NORTH SEA AND ENGLISH CHANNEL

THE ANGLO-DUTCH WARS OF THE 17TH CENTURY

English Miles

Map 42

"I knew if it could be done, it had to be done, and I did it."

—Gertrude Ederle

Gertrude Ederle was the first woman to swim across the English Channel, a strip of water twenty-one miles wide that runs between England and France. In the 1920s, people thought it was impossible for a woman to do such a thing. They thought women were too delicate. After several women had tried and failed, John Hayward wrote in the July 1926 *London Daily Sketch* that women should stop chasing this absurd dream. Since only five men had ever swum the Channel, what hope was there for a female to succeed?

In those days, women did not have track and field events in the Olympic Games because the Olympic Committee thought women were too weak for such events. Gertrude knew she was not frail. She was a strong swimmer. She knew she could do it no matter what other people thought.

Swimming for women was a pretty new sport in the 1920s. In 1915, Gertrude Ederle was a child learning to swim on the Jersey shore. Trudy considered

Gertrude Ederle Tidbits

◆ Trudy spent much of her life teaching swimming to deaf children in New York City.
◆ Ederle ate one chicken leg during her swim across the English Channel.

The official poster of the VIII Olympic Games held in Paris, France, in 1924.

Gertrude is honored for her historic swim and crowned "Queen of the Waves," September 8, 1926, New York City.

"Make yourself an example, achieve it, but don't hurt anyone on the way up."

—Dawn Fraser, three-time Olympic gold medal swimmer

herself a "water baby" since she took well to swimming. Doctors warned her to stop swimming or it would worsen a hearing problem she developed as a child, but she said, "I loved the water so much, I just couldn't stop."

As a teenager, Ederle started competitive swimming. Even though women in sports were barely tolerated, it was hard to ignore Gertrude. By the time she was eighteen, Trudy set twenty-nine United States and world records in swimming. She beat the records of both women and men. In the 1924 Olympic Games in Paris, Ederle took home one gold and two bronze medals. She was no longer a "water baby," she was a swimming champion.

After the Olympics, Trudy set her sights on the ultimate swimming challenge—to cross the English Channel. Thus far, five men had succeeded but no women. Two days before she left for France, Gertrude completed a marathon 22-mile swim across the New York harbor. She made it in seven hours and eleven minutes. A sportswriter of the time said, "There were few correspondents. There seemed to be some doubt as to whether this sort of thing came under the head of sports."

Ederle's first Channel attempt in 1925 did not pan out. After more than eight hours, one of the people in her spotting boat thought Trudy was unconscious. When they reached out and touched her, Ederle was disqualified. It turned out she was only resting. All Gertrude could think of was, "What will they think of me back in the States?"

Also in 1926

* The first waterproof watch is made in Switzerland.

* Harry Houdini, the magician, dies.

* WINNIE-THE-POOH is first published.

One year later, on August 6, 1926, Gertrude stepped onto the French shore again. She wore a red cap, goggles, and a two-piece bathing suit she and her sister had designed. The suit would have been scandalous in the United States. Trudy wasn't interested in scandal or bathing suit fashion; she wanted a suit that would cause less drag in the water. Slathered in grease to keep her warm in the frigid sea and to protect her skin from the saltwater, she entered the choppy waters and swam.

Fourteen hours and thirty-one minutes later, Ederle stepped onto the English shore to cheers from the waiting crowd. She had made it! She was the first woman to swim the English Channel. And she had set a new record. Not only was she the first woman, she was the fastest person. She had beaten the men's record by almost two hours. Trudy proved that women were not weak.

Back in the United States, she received a hero's welcome. Two million people lined the streets of New York City for a ticker tape parade in her honor. They chanted her name as a confetti snowstorm fell upon the swimmer. Because of her accomplishment, she was invited to the White House. President Coolidge called her "America's best girl." Gertrude's feat inspired many women of her time. One woman told the *New York Daily News* that Trudy's success would help women "become much stronger and self-reliant."

Gertrude Ederle proved women need not be weak—they could have STRENGTH, just like her.

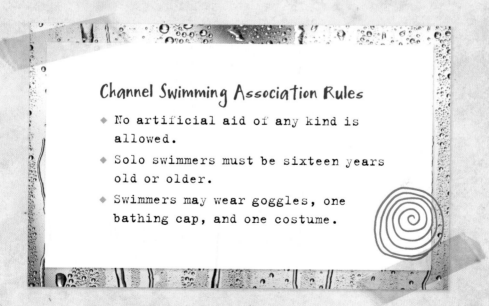

Channel Swimming Association Rules

- No artificial aid of any kind is allowed.
- Solo swimmers must be sixteen years old or older.
- Swimmers may wear goggles, one bathing cap, and one costume.

People should take challenges, especially older women who are often discouraged from it.

TENACITY
DR. DIANA HOFF

DR. DIANA HOFF
(b. 1944)

Have you ever looked at the ocean? You can't see the other side. It is thousands of miles before you reach the other shore. What type of woman would it take to climb into a rowboat to cross the ocean? Would she need stick-to-itness, or **TENACITY?** Yes.

Now imagine that it is your mother or your grandmother who chooses to cross that ocean. She is no longer young. Yet, she still needs strength. She also needs determination. That woman was Dr. Diana Hoff.

Diana Hoff rowed alone across the Atlantic Ocean when she was fifty-five. It took the Scotswoman 113 days. Diana Hoff didn't let someone tell her it wasn't the thing to do for a woman her age. She did it! And she made it across on January 5, 2000. She was the second woman to row across any ocean. The first woman, Tori

↖ After 3-and-a-half months at sea, Diana Hoff prepares to land at Port St. Charles, Barbados, to become the oldest person to row the Atlantic solo. Diana left the Canary Islands the same day as Kentucky lawyer Tori Murden, who became the first American and the first woman to cross the ocean solo when she reached the Caribbean island of Guadeloupe on December 3 after 81 days.

Dr. Diana Hoff Tidbits

◆ The STAR ATLANTIC II was the name of Diana's rowboat.
◆ Diana Hoff plays the viola and the violin.

Murden, beat her by a little over a month. Diana may have been the second woman, but she was the oldest person to ever row across an ocean. It wasn't easy. And not just because of her age or her gender, but because crossing an ocean in a rowboat for any human takes **TENACITY**.

On September 13, 1999, Diana Hoff and Tori Murden each climbed into her rowboat waiting in a small marina on the Canary Islands. Each hoped to become the first woman to row solo over the Atlantic Ocean or any ocean for that matter. Murden was thirty-six and a lawyer who lived in Louisville, Kentucky. Dr. Hoff was fifty-five and an eye specialist who lived in Norway. So far only men had succeeded in this endeavor. Now it was time for a woman.

"I felt it was a challenge. People should take challenges, especially older women who are often discouraged from it."
—Dr. Diana Hoff

They weren't the first females to try this ocean adventure. Six other attempts were met with failure. Murden tried to cross the Atlantic the year before but didn't make it. Diana Hoff's twenty-six-year-old daughter, Elizabeth, tried in February, but her boat capsized after ten days. This was Hoff's first try. The women smiled and waved as they headed out to sea. Both had over 3,000 miles of rowing to go.

Diana really wasn't much into rowing as a sport. She had rowed solo while she was at Glasgow University studying medicine. That is how she met her husband, Stein. He was in the rowing club and studying medicine just like Diana. But medical school was a long time ago, in the 1960s. Still, running marathons and sailing were hobbies of Diana's.

Diana had the sea in her blood. For Diana to choose to row the ocean was not out of character. She thought about her daughter and the other women who had failed in their attempts. She thought about Stein on a team row across the

Also in 1999

* Bertrand Piccard and Brian Jones become the first people to circle the Earth in a hot air balloon.

* Cathy O'Dowd, a South African mountaineer, becomes the first woman to summit Mount Everest from both the north and south sides.

ocean and thought, "Goodness this can't be that difficult." Diana and Stein built the boat she would use.

The crossing wasn't as easy as Diana believed it would be. Diana said, "Rowing a boat is a hopeless way of crossing an ocean. You can have no control over it when the wind and the current are against you." Rowing the waves was

Row Your Boat Records

- In 2004, Pavel Rezvoy of the Ukraine became the oldest oceanrower. He was sixty-five.
- On March 15, 2011, Suzanne Pinto, age fifty-eight, broke Diana's record for the oldest woman oceanrower.

- The youngest oceanrower is Rachel Flanders from Great Britain. In 2008, she crossed the Atlantic on a four-woman team. She was only seventeen!
- On December 3, 1999, Tori Murden became the first woman to row across an ocean. It took her eighty-two days.

like riding a wild bronco for hours. Sometimes the waves were so choppy, her oars stuck and she was thrown off of her seat. Yet, she continued to row. On most days Hoff rowed for ten hours.

It was just Diana with the sea and sky, but she wasn't completely alone. She watched a giant turtle eat barnacles off the bottom of her boat. Whales swam in the distance. One morning she found flying fish covering the deck of her boat. She e-mailed her husband each day. After over a month on the water, Diana saw her first humans. A cruise ship passed near enough so "the passengers and crew lined the rails." They cheered and applauded for Diana. They sent a life raft over with fresh fruit, books, and tapes. It would be over a month before she would see humans again.

After 112 days at sea, Diana Hoff saw land off the coast of Barbados. The sight was "far better than all of the beautiful sunsets and dawns" she witnessed over the last three and a half months. She heard faint music. It was an old pop song titled "Diana." Diana wrote in her journal, "I'm here! I've done it!" At that moment, Diana Hoff earned the honor of becoming the oldest person and the second woman to cross an ocean.

After rowing the ocean, Diana Hoff wrote, "I feel satisfied with what I have achieved." Diana Hoff completed what she set out to do. Diana Hoff has TENACITY.

SOURCES

Asterisk(*) = suitable for younger readers.

GUDRIDUR THORBJARNARDOTTIR

Brown, Nancy Marie. *The Far Traveler: Voyages of a Viking Woman.* Orlando: Harcourt, Inc., 2007.

Elphinstone, Margaret. *The Sea Road.* Edinburgh: Canongate Books, 2000.

Female Explorers Website. "Gudridur: Most Traveled Woman of the Middle Ages." http://www.squidoo.com/femaleexplorers.

The Globe and Mail's Website. Alanna Mitchell, "Icelanders Add a Leaf to Viking Mystery Tale." http://www.theglobeandmail.com/servlet/ArticleNews /PEstory/TGAM/20021130/USNORXI/International /international/internationalEuropeHeadline_temp/2/2/8.

Sailing West to Vinland Website. Bára Daðadóttir and Fríða Bjarnadóttir, "Gudridur Thorbjarnardottir." http://www.fva.is/~vinland/english/e_personur /e_gudridur.html.

SUSAN BUTCHER

Chamberlain, Tony. "Butcher Goal: Four in a Row." *Boston Globe*, March 18, 1988. Available from Highbeam Research, http://highbeam.com.

Trausch, Susan. "A Woman and Her Dogs." *Boston Globe*, October 18, 1987. Available from Highbeam Research, http://highbeam.com.

Brennan, Patricia. "Iditarod's Super Musher; Susan Butcher Hits the Trail." *Washington Post*, March 5, 1989. Available from Highbeam Research, http://highbeam.com.

Chamberlain, Tony. "Mushing Is What Butcher Likes Doing Best." *Boston Globe*, March 16, 1990. Available from Highbeam Research, http://highbeam.com.

Iditarod's Website http://iditarod.com/learn/trivia.html.

KIT DESLAURIERS

DesLauriers, Kit. "I Skied Down Mt. Everest." *Redbook*, October 1, 2007. Available from Highbeam Research, http://highbeam.com.

American Way Magazine's Website. Joseph Guinto, "One Woman, Seven Summits." http://www.americanwaymag.com /rob-deslauriers-everest-skiing-jackson-hole.

CBS News's Website. Brian Dakss, "First Woman Skis Mount Everest." http://www.cbsnews.com/stories/2006/12/27 /earlyshow/main2302288.shtml.

ESPN's Website. Tom Rinaldi, "Breaking Barriers: DesLauriers' Descents from the Tops of the World." http://sports.espn.go.com/espn/news /story?page=080206deslauriers.

Kit DesLauriers's Home Page. http://www.kitdski.com.

NPR Website. Melissa Block, "Women Skier Conquers Everest, 'Seven Summits.'" http://www.npr.org/templates/story /story.php?storyId=6368913.

Outside Online Website. Dave Hahn, "The No Fall Zone." January 2007 issue. http://outside.away.com/outside/destinations/200701 /skiing-everest_1.html.

VALENTINA TERESHKOVA

Tereshkova, Valentina. "The First Lady of Space Remembers: Excerpts from Valentina Tereshkova's Memoirs, *Stars Are Calling*, Moscow, 1964." *Quest*, November 10, 2003.

Encyclopedia Astronautica Website. "Tereshkova." http://www.astronautix.com/astros/terhkova.htm.

Encyclopedia of World Biography Website. "Valentina Tereshkova Biography." http://www.notable biographies.com/St-Tr/Tereshkova-Valentina.html.

SOURCES

BESSIE COLEMAN

*Hart, Philip S. *Up in the Air: The Story of Bessie Coleman*. Minneapolis: Carolrhoda Books, Inc., 1996.

McLean, Jacqueline. *Women with Wings*. Minneapolis: The Oliver Press, Inc., 2001.

Boustany, Nora. "A Down-to-Earth Highflier." *Washington Post*, March 24, 2006.

McAllister, Bill. "Heritage Series, Flying High." *Washington Post*, April 7, 1995. Available from Highbeam Research, http://highbeam.com.

Warner-Rotzoll, Brenda. "A Soaring Role Model." *Chicago Sun-Times*, March 25, 2003. Available from Highbeam Research, http://highbeam.com.

Kisor, Henry. "Bessie Coleman Flew in the Face of Racial Stereotypes." *Chicago Sun-Times*, August 29, 1993. Available from Highbeam Research, http://highbeam.com.

*Sutcliffe, Jane. "Fly High, Bessie Coleman." *Highlights for Children*, February 1, 2004. Available from Highbeam Research, http://highbeam.com.

Ivery, Ribin. "Bessie Coleman, the First Black Woman Aviator." *Miami Times*, March 19, 2002. Available from Highbeam Research, http://highbeam.com.

Jackson, David Earl. "Dare-Devil Bessie Coleman Honored." *Tri-State Defender,* December 13, 1995. Available from Highbeam Research, http://highbeam.com.

McCoy, Lezlie B. "Bessie Coleman: From Cotton-Picker to Queen of Aviation." *Philadelphia Tribune*, December 9, 2003. Available from Highbeam Research, http://highbeam.com.

Hargrave: *Aviation and Aeromodelling—Interdependent Evolutions and Histories.* "The Pioneers: Elizabeth 'Bessie' Coleman (1893–1926)." http://www.ctie.monash.edu.au/hargrave/coleman_bio.html.

JANET GUTHRIE

Guthrie, Janet. *Janet Guthrie: A Life at Full Throttle*. Toronto: Sport Media Publishing, Inc., 2005.

Conceptcarz.com Website. "1975 Lightning Indy Racer." http://www.conceptcarz.com/vehicle/z14507/Lightning-Indy-Racer.aspx.

Janet Guthrie's Home Page. "Janet Guthrie Biography." http://www.janetguthrie.com/biofr.htm.

AMELIA EARHART

*Burleigh, Robert. *Amelia Earhart Free in the Skies*. Orlando: Harcourt, Inc., 2003.

*Szabo, Corinne. *Sky Pioneer: A Photobiography of Amelia Earhart*. Washington DC: National Geographic, 1997.

*Lauber, Patricia. *Lost Star: The Story of Amelia Earhart*. New York: Scholastic Inc., 1988.

*Bull, Angela. *Flying Ace: The Story of Amelia Earhart*. New York: DK Publishing, Inc., 2000.

Official Amelia Earhart Website. "Biography." http://www.ameliaearhart.com/about/biography.htm.

SOPHIE BLANCHARD

Donn, Linda. *The Little Balloonist*. New York: Plume, 2006.

Hilton Hightower's Blog. "It's Electric Times Sophie Blanchard!" http://hiltonhightower.blogspot.com.

Kittybrewster.com Website. "Norwich Duff: Journal Extract on the Death of La Veuve Blanchard." http://www.kittybrewster.com/images/Norwich_Duff_Journal_pages017to018.htm.

University of Houston's Website. John H. Lienhard, "Women in Flight: Balloons, Parachutes, Airplanes, and the Search for Equity." This talk was presented at *The Breakfast Club*, River Oaks Country Club on January 20, 1999. http://uh.edu/engines/womfly.htm.

NELLIE BLY

*Fredeen, Charles. *Nellie Bly: Daredevil Reporter*. Minneapolis: Lerner, 2000.

Bly, Nellie. *Around the World in Seventy-Two Days*. New York: The Pictorial Weeklies Company, 1890. Available from University of Pennsylvania, http://digital.library.upenn.edu.

Bly, Nellie. *Ten Days in a Mad-House*. New York: Ian L. Muro, n.d. Available from University of Pennsylvania, http://digital.library.upenn.edu.

New York Correction Historical Society's Website. Excerpt from Brooke Kroeger's *Nellie Bly: Daredevil, Reporter, Feminist*. Published by Times Books. http://www.correctionhistory.org/rooseveltisland/bly/html/preblackwell.html.

MARGARET BOURKE-WHITE

Bourke-White, Margaret. *Portrait of Myself*. New York: Simon and Schuster, 1963.

Masters of Photography Website. Excerpt from Sean Callahan's *Margaret Bourke-White: Photographer*. Published by Bulfinch Press. http://www.masters-of-photography.com/B/bourke-white/b-w_articles3.html.

Photographing the Representative American: Margaret Bourke-White in the Depression Website. http://xroads.virginia.edu/~CLASS/am485_98/coe/photofrnt.html.

SmartWomenInvest.com Website. Austin Hendrix, "Margaret Bourke-White, Photo Journalist, 1906–1971." http://www.smartwomeninvest.com/peoplepics.htm.

GERTRUDE EDERLE

*Adler, David. "America's Champion Swimmer." *Children's Digest*, April 1, 2001. Available from Highbeam Research, http://highbeam.com.

Severo, Richard. "Gertrude Ederle, the First Woman to Swim Across the English Channel, Dies at 98." *New York Times*, December 1, 2003. Available from Highbeam Research, http://highbeam.com.

Severo, Richard. "Channel Swimmer Outdid Men and Won Hearts." *International Herald Tribune*, December 2, 2003. Available from Highbeam Research, http://highbeam.com.

Sport Heroes of the 1920s Website. Melissa Grawburg, "A Look at Gertrude Ederle." https://www.msu.edu/~grawbur1/iahweb.html.

Telegraph's Website. Gavin Mortimer, "When Gertrude Ederle Turned the Tide." http://www.telegraph.co.uk/culture/donotmigrate/3672954/When-Gertrude-Ederle-turned-the-tide.html.

DR. DIANA HOFF

Hoff, Diana and Nathalie Curry. "My Week: Diana Hoff Aged 55 the British Oarswoman Became the Oldest Person Ever to Row Across an Ocean When She Completed Her Crossing of the Atlantic on Wednesday." *Independent-London*, January 8, 2000. Available from Highbeam Research, http://highbeam.com.

Houston, Simon. "Diana's One in a Row." *Daily Record* (Glasgow, Scotland), January 6, 2000. Available from Highbeam Research, http://highbeam.com.

BBC News's Website. "Go Girls: Women Adventurers." http://news.bbc.co.uk/1/hi/uk/592211.stm.

Diana Hoff's Home Page. http://www.whiteadmiral.com/aboutdands.htm.

GENERAL

*Saari, Peggy. *Prominent Women of the 20th Century*. New York: Gale Research, Inc., 1996.

*Kimmel, Elizabeth Cody. *Ladies First: 40 Daring American Women Who Were Second to None*. Washington DC: National Geographic, 2006.

Bennett, Arnold. *Our Women*. New York: George H. Doran Company, 1920.

Trager, James. *The People's Chronology: A Year-by-Year Record of Human Events from Prehistory to the Present*. New York: Henry Holt and Company, 1992.

Grun, Bernard. *The Timetables of History*. New York: Simon and Schuster, 1963.

Ash, Russell. *Fantastic Millennium Facts*. Willowdale, Ontario: Firefly Books, 1999.

CREDITS

Front cover:

Amelia Earhart: Keystone-France/Gamma-Keystone/Getty Images;
Janet Guthrie: Racing One/ISC Archives/Getty Images

Back cover:

Viking pendant: © iStockphoto.com/Cindy England

Art elements repeated throughout book:

Background paper: © iStockphoto.com/Mike Bentley
Green watercolor brush marks: © iStockphoto.com/Scott Waite
Illustrated frames and dingbats: © iStockphoto.com/UteHil
Photo corners: © iStockphoto.com/Samantha Grandy
Spiral notebook: © iStockphoto.com/Stefanie Timmermann
Tape edges: © iStockphoto.com/Florea Marius Catali
Yellow sticky notes: © iStockphoto.com/Robyn Mackenzie
White notes: © iStockphoto.com/Robyn Mackenzie

GUDRIDUR THORBJARNARDOTTIR

p. 9 top right: The Jamestown Yorktown Collection, Williamsburg, Va. USA. Photograph courtesy of The Bridgeman Art Library.

p. 9 bottom left: Arnamagnaean Collection, Denmark/The Bridgeman Art Library.

p. 10 top: Map from *Viking Tales* by Jennie Hall (1875–1921). Chicago & New York: Rand McNally, 1902.

p. 10 bottom: Photograph by Lynn E. Noel © 2004 www.lynnoel.com. *The first white mother in America*, 1938, Ásmundur Sveinsson © heirs of Ásmundur Sveinsson/Myndstef 2011

p. 12: Viking pendant: © iStockphoto.com/Cindy England

p. 13: Fire crackers: © iStockphoto.com/Jaap2

SUSAN BUTCHER

p. 14: © iStockphoto.com/Matt Cooper

p. 15 left: Reprinted with the permission of the Iditarod Trail Committee, Inc.

p. 15 right: © 2011 by Jeff Schultz/AlaskaStock.com

p. 16: AP Photo/*Anchorage Daily News*, Bill Roth

p. 17: William R. Sallaz/*Sports Illustrated*/Getty Images

p. 18: Dog biscuit: © iStockphoto.com/Imagesbybarbara

p. 21: © Jon Van Zyle

KIT DESLAURIERS

pp. 22, 26 inset, 28: © Jimmy Chin

p. 23: Skis: © iStockphoto.com/David Morgan

p. 25: Empire State Building: © iStockphoto.com/David Dang

pp. 26–27: Mount Everest: © iStockphoto.com/Grazyna Niedzieska

VALENTINA TERESHKOVA

p. 31: Keystone/Hulton Archive/Getty Images

pp. 33, 35: © RIA Novosti/Alamy

BESSIE COLEMAN

pp. 36, 38: Michael Ochs Archives/Getty Images

p. 37: Fotosearch/Archive Photos/Getty Images

pp. 40, 41 top: Used with the permission of the *Chicago Defender*

p. 41 bottom: National Air and Space Museum, Smithsonian Institution (SI 99-15416)

p. 42: Baseball: © iStockphoto.com/ranplett

JANET GUTHRIE

p. 44 top: AP Photo

p. 44 bottom: AP Photo/Lowe's Motor Speedway

pp. 45, 49: Racing One/ISC Archives/Getty Images

p. 47: AP Photo/Marty Lederhandler

AMELIA EARHART

pp. 50, 53, 54 bottom, 57 top: AP Photo

p. 51: Pictures Inc./Time & Life Pictures/Getty Images

p. 52: *NY Daily News* Archive /Getty Images

p. 54: Portrait: Keystone-France/Gamma-Keystone/Getty Images

p. 57: Newspaper: Reproduced with permission of the Baltimore Sun Company from *The Evening Sun*, front page, July 3, 1937, permission conveyed through Copyright Clearance Center, Inc.

SOPHIE BLANCHARD

pp. 59 bottom left, 63 top left: Library of Congress Prints and Photographs Division

pp. 59 top right, 63 bottom right: Apic/Hulton Archive/Getty Images

p. 60: © Science Museum Pictorial/Science and Society Picture Library

pp. 61, 62: "It's Electric Times, Sophie Blanchard," used with permission of the author, Hilton Hightower © 2007

NELLIE BLY

pp. 64, 65, 70: Library of Congress Prints and Photographs Division

p. 67: Picture Collection, The New York Public Library, Astor, Lenox and Tilden Foundations

p. 68: Library of Congress Newspaper and Periodicals Reading Room

p. 69: Hulton Archive/Getty Images

MARGARET BOURKE-WHITE

p. 72: Oscar Graubner/Time & Life Pictures /Getty Images

pp. 73, 74 bottom, 76: Margaret Bourke-White /Time & Life Pictures/Getty Images

p. 74 top: Time Inc. Picture Collection/Time & Life Pictures/Getty Images

GERTRUDE EDERLE

pp. 79, 80 top left and top right, 82 top: AP Photo

p. 80 bottom: University of Texas Libraries

p. 81: Fried chicken: © iStockphoto.com /oytun karadayi

p. 82 bottom: Topical Press Agency /Hulton Archive/Getty Images

p. 85: Water texture: © iStockphoto.com/sidsnapper

DR. DIANA HOFF

pp. 86, 87: AP Photo/Willie Alleyne

p. 88: Viola and violin: © iStockphoto.com /Laura Frenkel

p. 90: Paddle: © iStockphoto.com/pixhook